Ancient Sun God

Professor Hilton Hotema

ISBN: 978-1-63923-126-3

Printed: January 2022

Cover Art By: Paul Amid

Published and Distributed By:
Lushena Books
607 Country Club Drive, Unit E
Bensenville, IL 60106
www.lushenabks.com

ISBN: 978-1-63923-126-3

The Ancient Sun God

Prof. Hilton Hotema

Table of Contents

Chapter No.1
The Ancient Light

Always there is a LIGHT in the humble hut in the Eastern Hemisphere, — a LIGHT that never, fails, either physically or symbolically. To that extent the Roman Catholic Church has been unable to eradicate all traces of the Ancient Sun worship of the Masters. Moreover, it adopted that same symbol of Solar Worship to please its members and to increase their number.

A LIGHT constantly burns over the Altar of the church. A LIGHT constantly burns before the Holy Ark in the synagogue. There is a LIGHT illuminating the Crescent of the mosque. There was a LIGHT upon the hearth in ancient days.

With the ancient Masters, Fire Worship evolved from sun worship, and had its symbolical meaning. It is the oldest of all forms of ancient religion.

Fire was venerated as a symbol of the Sun, that Mighty Luminary from which all things emanate, and to which, said the masters, all things return. Pyra is Greek for fire, or light, or the illumination that reveals something or makes things visible in the dark, as well as giving heat.

Midos in Greek and means "measures." So the word pyramid is a combination of the Greek words Pyra and Midos; and the Greeks adopted them from the phoenician word "purimmiddah," which means "light-measures." The pyramid is an ancient symbol constitutes measured revelations, or revelations through measurements.

Christian authors have twisted everything about the great pyramid of Gizeh to make it appear as an Altar of Stone to the Church of God in the midst of Egypt.

In shape, the pyramid represents the ascending flame, flying upward to meet its Divine Original, — a symbol of the Eternal Spark of Life and Death, the origin and the end of the One Flame. It is Life and Death, the origin and the end of every material thing.

Fire is the most ancient symbol of Life. It is a symbol of the purity of the Cosmic Elements. The purifying power of fire is naturally deducted from this symbol of the purity of the element. In the Egyptian Mysteries there was a symbolical "purification by fire," as stated in our work *Mysterious Sphinx*. In the bible appears many references to the second fire. God appeared to Moses in a flame of fire descended from heaven to consume the burnt-offering.

The fire philosophers espoused the veneration of fire, and cultivated the "Fire Secret," not as an idolatrous practice, but modified by their Hermetic doctrines. They were also called "Theosophists," and through them, or in reference to them, the Theosophic Degrees of Freemasonry came into existence in the 18th century.

As fire and light are regarded as synonymous, so is the fire, which was to the Zoroastrians the symbol that concealed one of their deeper secrets. That secret we have revealed in our series of works listed in the back of *The Mysterious Sphinx*.

Our Star Sun

Out local sun, with its attendant planets, is moving through space at a speed of 200 miles a second, traveling around the center to make a complete revolution of its gigantic orbit.

How many times the Sun have circled its orbit cannot be determined nor even accurately estimated. According to some authorities it must have made thousands, and perhaps hundreds of thousands, of complete revolutions. The earth's diameter is about 7,290 miles, but that of the sun is over a hundred times as great. Mathematicians assert that the Sun's mass is 332,000 times of that of the earth. The Sun's heat is enormous, and several interesting calculations have been made in an attempt to illustrate it.

For example, it has been determined that if the whole of the solar radiation could be concentrated on a solid column of ice nearly three miles in diameter, stretching from the earth to the Sun, about 93,000,000 miles, it would melt in one second, and the resulting water would be transformed to steam in not more than eight seconds.

The shatterproof reflector, used in certain searchlights on the U.S Navy's largest battleships can generate so much heat by concentration of light, that if it is placed so as to gather the sun's rays, a metal nail suspended at a focal point will melt.

For many years the attention of inventors has been directed to the question of utilizing the direct rays of the sun as a substitute for coal, wood, or other fuel; large burning-glasses or reflectors being the general form of the various machines.

A so called burning mirror made in France by Villette, was four feet in diameter and produced heat too intense that, according to the report, it melted cast iron in 16 seconds.

The press of March 25, 1956 reported that, "in violence equal to 100,000,000 H-bombs exploding all at once, the sun suddenly shot a tongue of flaming gas into space."

One billion tons of the Sun's mass of gases were expelled. A huge knot of gas shot away 700 miles per second, or at 2,500,000 miles per hour. All this, some movies showed today, was what happened last February 10, when astronomers reported a "remarkable occurrence" on the sun, a record flare rising in fire from the Sun's edge.

The movies were taken with a coronagraph, a special instrument kept trained on the Sun, to study flares, at the Air Force Sacramento Peak Observatory in New Mexico.

First came a bubble of gas, expanding at 60 miles per second, on the eastern edge of the sun. It grew steadily more brilliant for five to ten minutes. Then suddenly a top knot of the bubble sped up to 700 miles per second. This knot, about 20,00 miles in diameter, shot out 200,000 miles before becoming too dim to see. Most of the gas expelled was hydrogen.

The ultraviolet light force from the flare played hob with radio transmission for a time by affecting the ionosphere which usually bounces radio waves back to earth.

The cause of the sun-flares is not fully known. They could be caused by shock waves from tremendous upsurges of gases in the sun's atmosphere. Or due to electrical and magnetic forces near and active sunspot group. Recent discoveries reveal the fact that there is a peculiar magnetism in the air which the Germans used to operate magnetic mines.

Dr. Felix Ehrenhaft, of New York, read a paper on the subject to the American Physical Society meeting in Columbus, Ohio, and reported in the press of June 17, 1945. Ehrenhaft said:

"Sunlight magnetism is equal to about one-fifth of the earth's magnetic force, which guides compass needles, and was used by the Germans to operate magnetic mines.

He showed photographs of iron particles in rapid spiral motion due to magnetism in sunlight. The iron particles, each about the diameter of a wavelength of life, floated in the sunlight. The camera showed that these bits of iron traveled horizontally thru the air toward the sun. Not only iron, but other metals, smoke particles, and all organic particles spiraled in the magnetic force of sunlight...

He suggested that the discovery (of this secret of the air) may explain in part why the Sun has lasted so long without cooling. It is fed the the sub-microscopic particles from space riding in the magnetism in light. The spiraling caused by the magnetism of light could be the basis of the universal whirling motion of everything in creation, earth, sun, stars, nebulae, galaxies, atoms, and molecules.

Dana Howard, in April-1944 issue of American Astrology, looks to the great ocean of spiritual Essence for power that will regenerate man. He wrote:

"Regeneration must be brought about on a universal scale. That is not beyond the pale of possibility; for underlying the depravity of world-misery, there is (in the air) a gigantic healing power yet untapped.

"Our astrological forefathers stumbled upon it intuitively; but it belongs to the coming of the 'Air Age' to make it a reality. These long-whiskered men of wisdom knew that the planets are in communion with the planetary chemical natures."

Howard then discusses planetary and Atmospheric Chemistry, and asserts that modern science has gone to sleep because it fails to study the Atmospheric soil, in which is deeply buried the "Virility of all life." He refers to the mysterious element in the air termed ozone, and mentions its effect on the blood and body, stating:

"One of the largest ozonating systems to be found is in the central London railway. It is recorded that during a severe influenza epidemic, motor drivers who ran thru the tubes daily were free of the disorder. In a small way ozone is being used in hospitals, public schools, and in the sterilization of water systems. But the fact remains that it is still in the embryonic stages of development. The average man has never heard of Ozone, except as an element present in the atmosphere after an electric storm, or in connection with the mountains or seashore.

More information concerning magnetism contained in the spiritual essence appears in reports concerning the mysterious "flying saucers."

Since 1947 reports have appeared from the time to time in this daily press regarding these strange objects in the air, concerning which no one seems to know anything definitely.

It appears that one Frank Scully has written a book on the subject. A short review of which appears in the Grit of October 15, 1950, from which we quote:

"Flying saucers have landed on the earth from some distant planet. They are disk-shaped machines made of metal lighter than aluminum but stronger than steel. They move by magnetic power. Their crews are men only three or three and a half feet high, who, expect for their shortness, look like ordinary human beings, they live on the tablets that contain an unknown kind of concentrated food. The saucers are not armed, but they do contain scientific apparatus, including a type of radio unknown on this earth.

"There is still hope that air forces officials may decide that we, the people, are worth taking into confidence. Flying saucers were first reported June 25, 1947, by Kenneth Arnold. Thousands of such reports have been made since then.

"Scully reports that a team of scientists made an examination of a saucer-like spaceship that landed near Aztec, N. M. Inside it were 16 dead men, regarded from 36 to 42 inches in height. The bodies were normal from every standpoint.

"The ship was about 100 feet in diameter, with round cabin 18 feet in diameter and 72 inches high. There was a panel of push buttons and instrument which the scientists could not understand. The scientists concluded that the ship flew on mysterious lines of magnetic force. They reasoned also that its landing was probably an accident that reunited from some disturbance of the magnetic field in which the craft operated.

"Three other ships landed in the country later, Scully says, and all have been studied by air force experts. The air forces he's never satisfactory explained the following incidents:

"A report by two veteran Eastern airline pilots that they saw a flame-shooting space ship near Montgomery, Alabama in July 1948. Or the strange death of Capt. Thomas F. Mantell, of the air force, who reported during a routine flight

Jan. 7 1948, that he was in pursuit of a spaceship over Ft. Knox, Ky. That was the last heard of him. His body was later found in the wreckage of his plane near Ft. Knox.

"Scully states that in his book that a scientist who lectured in the University of Denver, told in complex language how a spaceship moving on magnetic power would also be able to demagnetize any object in its path, thus causing its immediate destruction."

Chapter No. 2
The Great Sun

When the writings of the ancient world were destroyed by the founders of the Roman Catholic Church, they kept and concealed that record of astronomical observations which went back into the night of time for more than half a million years.

That precious record, now carefully concealed in the Vatican library from the eyes of a deceived world, contains a startling account of the Great Central Sun, termed by the Masters as the "Sun Behind the Sun," and concerning which modern science knows nothing.

The existence of the Great Sun was known in all ages but the present, and is known now to occult scientist. We regard our local sun as a huge body, and it is. The great red giant, Antares (Alpha Scorpii), is so large that its mass is some hundreds of thousands of time that of our sun. It has 4,000 times the candle-power of our sun, and is over 450 times its diameter.

So huge is Antares that it would require 53.3 minutes for an electric current to travel halfway around it. The brightest star (sun) now known in the universe is S. Doradus; 500,000 times brighter than our Sun. It is far beyond the milky way, in the star family known as the large magellanic cloud. It is visible only in telescopes.

The biggest stars exceed the radius of the planet Jupiter's orbit. That is, if one these stars replaced our local Sun,

Jupiter, about 470,000,000 miles from our sun, would be inside the star.

There are eight known of this size or bigger. The largest has a diameter of a billion seven hundred million miles. These calculations are by Dr. Barlow Shapley, director of the Harvard College Observatory, in the journal, proceedings of the National Academy of Sciences.

Influence of the Great Sun

It is said that the beneficent influence flowing from the Great Sun is such, that the solar force radiating into humanity at these propitious periods of time, enables the adept to awaken the format organs, channels, and nerve plexi without his body, which causes his seven stars (seven great nerve centers), symbolically termed the seven eyes of the Lord which run to and fro through the whole earth (body — Zech. 4:1), to Glo-ray (glorify) as centers of spiritual light (Jn. 1:9 15;5), and to function on a higher plane of consciousness.

Man is an epitome of the Universe. Each body cell is a replica of the Universe. Within each cell there is an Intelligent Life Point — the sun (nucleus) of the Cell Universe, which. Like our physical sun, receives light and life from the local sun and also from the sun behind the sun.

The ancient engineers who designed and built the Great Pyramid of Gizeh, had knowledge of the Great Sun, which the Atlanteans had names Usiris — Sirius, Dog star.

The ancient engineers knew that once a year the Great Sun is in line with Sirius. For that reason the Pyramid was so built that, at the precise moment; light of Sirius (Usirius) fell on the square (Divine Stone), which was placed at the upper end of the Grand Gallery, so that the light shone on the Great Hierophant, "who received the Super Solar Force, and sought, through his own perfected body, to transmit to the initiates this added invigoration of the evolution of their Divinity. This was the secret purpose of the Square Divine Stone, whereon, in the ritual, Osiris sits to bestow upon the Illuminate the Crown of Celestial Light and Glory.

The "Sun behind the Sun," mentioned above, is allegorically referred to in the Bible. It is described as a chariot of fire and horses of fire: "Behold, there appeared a chariot of fire, and Horses of Fire...and Elijah went up into heaven by a whirlwind" (2 Kings 2:11).

According to the legend, when the Great Sun comes into conjunction with our local sun, there occurs a reign of extraordinary awakening and effusion of light throughout our entire solar system, and it affects more or less everything on the earth

As the superpower of the Great Sun is transmitted to the earth through our local Sun, "it is said to send greater power into the consciousness of the earth sphere, that a New Era of Thought and Intelligence may be born in the minds of men for the stimulation and guidance of Spiritual Development.

That event is badly needed now, in order to dissipate the reign of materialism with which mankind has been cursed since the dawn of Evolutionism, but it will not occur if there is any way in which theology or science can prevent.

The birth of evolutionism resulted directly from the fact, that intelligent men could not swallow the personal god of the church, and his son Jesus. Evolutionism is the child of science which admits almost total ignorance of the constitution of Man.

Alexis Carrel, one of the great scientists of modern times, declared that "our ignorance (of man) is profound. Most of the questions put to themselves by those who study human beings remain without answer" (Man The Unknown, p.4).

Chapter No.3
Secret Of The Stars

Europe and America have little reliable history of the ancient world. That history was destroyed by the church in the 4th and 5th centuries, when it burned the big libraries. Then the church fathers wrote their own history of the ancient world, and that is the history contained in encyclopedias. Much of it is false, incorrect, and misleading.

That is the reason why we find no correct account of the ancient masters and their wonderful work, and why their three great symbols, the Zodiac, the Sphinx, and the Caduceus, receive such scanty and faulty mention.

Dictionaries and encyclopedias purposely fail to tell us that the Zodiac Circle, those mysterious wheels of the Ezekiel (1:15,16), with its twelve points, reveals, explains and proves the arrangement and composition of the Universe, and the place of everything in it.

The symbolism of the Zodiac applied to everything kind of force, matter, and element in the Universe, from the primordial unit of fire to the Supreme Intelligence of the Cosmos.

It shows the composition and position of man in relation to everything above and below, inside and outside. It shows that man is the pivot, the fulcrum, the balance wheel and the microcosm of the material world. It shows that everything contained in the universe is contained in men. The twelve zodiac marks are the elements of a language that surpasses in accuracy and with which jargon of philosophy cannot be compared.

The twelve points for which the names stand, are the principles of a science as certain as mathematics, and as startling as the modern discovery of the Endocrine System of a man's body.

The zodiac is the great symbol of the masters through which man can come in contact with ancient wisdom that he has lost — wisdom that has been destroyed by the church, the despots and tyrants of past ages.

The passages of the Sun through the Twelve Signs of the Zodiac was the basis of the Science of the Masters, who studied the trail of man as traveling through the "Twelve Houses of Polarities (many mansions — Jn. 14:2,3) of the Zodiac during the days of his earthly existence, and, in each house, experiencing a valuable lesson.

In its great circuit, the earth passes through the range of a Constellation, represented by a circle of 2,160 years. During that period of time, the annual birth of the Sun (December 25) occurs in the same zodiac sign. In each Grand cycle of 25,868 years, the Earth passes passes through all the Twelve Houses just as the sun goes through them in 365.26 days.

Cicero declared that the Chaldeans had records of the stars for a space of 37,000 years. Epigenes, Berosus and Critodemes set the duration of astronomical observations by the Babylonians at from 490,000 to 720,000 years (Thorndyke). Others assert that still older records were brought to Egypt by Seth, Enoch, Noah and Shem.

Cicero asserted that, over a period of thousands of years, the Chaldeans kept the nativities (horoscopes) of all children born among them, and from this huge mass of data, calculated the effects on man of the various planets of the zodiac signs.

The science of the Stars was not developed as a dogmatic belief, nor to support a preconceived theory, but derived its establishment from thousands of years of careful observation by philosophers of the highest order.

Ezekiel's Wheels

"A whirlwind came out of the north, and a great cloud — Behold one wheel upon the earth — and their appearance and their work was, as it were, a wheel in the middle of a wheel — and when the living creatures were lifted up from the earth, the wheels were lifted up — For the spirit of the living creatures was in the wheels."

For emphasis, the last sentence was repeated: "For the spirit of living creatures was in the wheels" (Ezek. 1:15, 16). Ezekiel's wheels are the Zodiac, and they deal with the astrological doctrine of the ascending Macrocosmos and the descending Microcosmos.

The same is true of Jacob's ladder — six steps up from Libra to Aries, and six steps down on the other side from Aries to Libra.

"And he dreamed, and beheld a ladder set up on the earth, and the top of it reaching to heaven; and behold the angels of God ascending and descending on it" (Gen. 28:12)

The angels symbolize the ascending Macrocosmos and descending Microcosmos. The grand cycle of the spirit; the

Wheel of Fortune, Tarot Card 11, mentioned in Chapter 11 of our work "Cosmic Creation."

Precession of the Equinoxes

The Sun does not arrive at the same moment each year at the equinoctial point of the equator. The result of this is termed the Precession of the Equinoxes.

This is a retrograde motion in the passage of our local Sun as it crosses the ecliptic each year, and means that the Sun is constantly changing its position in the Zodiac at each vernal equinox. The annual amount of precession is a little over 50 seconds, and amounts to 30 degrees, or a sign of the Zodiac, in 2,160 years; and the particular change we are now experiencing, will not occur again for 25,868 years. That is the reason why the Masters, thousands of years ago, divided the zodiac circle into 30 degrees. We shall presently see how modern science "saves face" by concealing this ancient knowledge.

It will readily be observed that it required a vast period of time for the masters to check and recheck this data through ages in order to formulate their changes and make their records, showing and describing not only these mysteries of the universe, but also the states and conditions of the earth and its inhabitants, as affected and influenced by the different variations of the various celestial bodies symbolize in the zodiac, — all of which the dictionary and encyclopedias declare is false, counterfeit and spurious.

When the histories, encyclopedias and the works of modern science state that the Zodiac "seems to have originated with the Chaldean astronomers about 2100 B.C." the authors of such statements are either lying, or are ignorant of the facts, and are not competent to write on the subject.

As further evidence of the flagrant manner in which reputable publications are distorted to conceal the facts and hide the knowledge of the Masters, it is stated in *"Marvels and Mysteries of Science,"* published in 1941, that Hipparchus discovered the precession of the equinoxes" in 125 B.C. we quote:

"The Greek astronomer, Hipparchus, who has been called the father of astronomy, in 125 B.C. discovered the precession of the equinoxes by comparing the length of the year, determined by dates when certain bright stars could first be seen in the dawn after the sun had passes them in its annual motion, with the length of the year of the seasons determined with the gnomon.

"This amazing discovery of motion of the earth that requires nearly 26,000 years for the completion of one circuit, sometimes called the Great Year, could not be explained at the time, but had to wait 1800 years for the mind of Newton to explain the physical cause" (p.viii).

Lies and falsehoods. The statement that Hipparchus made "this amazing discovery" is false, and made to "save face" and protect the reputation of science. Also to boost "the mind of Newton." That amazing discovery" was made by the Masters half of a million years ago, and the knowledge was lost when Romanism destroyed the ancient records.

Chapter No.4
Astrology Changed To Astronomy

The beginnings of astrology are lost in the night of time. It was practiced by the very earliest people on earth, and the science emerges, in a highly developed state, from the utter obscurity of the ancient world.

The ancient Egyptians maintained that the science of astrology was bestowed upon man by the benevolence of the gods. The elder nations of the earth conceded the Egyptian premise.

Astrology was practiced in India thousands of years before the compiling of the Vedas. The great magician and astrologer, Asuramaya, was said to have been born in Atlantis, thus testifying, upon the authorities of the Puranas, to the extreme antiquity of this celestial science (Blavatsky).

After Romanism had fanatically destroyed the ancient records of astrology, it was a matter of courting death by burning during the dark ages for a man to attempt to revive the work.

Wm. McCarthy wrote: "For more than 1200 years, the church rejected all science and murdered all who attempted to explain anything except through the supernatural and miraculous. Even today, where a scientific fact, conflicts with the Bible or a belief of the church, the church has decreed that the scientific fact must yield to faith" (Bible, Church and God, P.121).

Astrology preserved itself by going "underground," and, to appease Romanism, the study of the stars became "astronomy," and attention was centered only on the physical composition of the cosmos., utterly disregarding the spiritual aspect for fear of the wrath of the church.

In further appeasement of Romanism, modern science perverted the application of knowledge from its legitimate ends, thus making astronomy a purely abstract and, to the delight of the church, a comparatively useless study, so far man is concerned.

For astronomy, as now presented, can contribute little more than tables of meaningless figures to a world that is bankrupt in spiritual, philosophical, intellectual and ethical values as a result of a spurious religious system that is as false as it is counterfeit.

Astrology was scientific theology with the Masters. It dealt with the cosmic effect of the stars and planets upon the earth, nature, and men.

The twelve signs of the Zodiac have always been arranged to represent the physical form of man, and to tell, symbolically, the story of Spiritual Man in relation to Physical Man.

The masters recognized man's physical form as but an instrument of breath, vibration, activated by cosmic radiation — waves of light and sound, and positive and negative electromagnetic forces in limitless action.

While astrology has been ridiculed and condemned by the church and by science as just another example of heathenish superstition, science now presents the announcement of certain discoveries that confirm everything that the Masters ever claimed for astrology.

Science has found a forced termed Cosmic Radiation, which consists of vibratory rays, waves, and beams, filling all space and so powerful and penetrating that they pass entirely through the earth and all other objects, affecting more or less all bodies with which they come in contact, including every cell and organ in the body.

These late findings confirm in its entirety the whole doctrine taught by the Masters for thousands of years before Romanism was ever born. These late discoveries show that from the infinitesimally small to the infinitesimally great, every part of the universe affects and acts upon every other part, just exactly as the masters taught.

Berman states that evidence has been discovered of the existence of a sex (propagative) rhythm in the phases of the moon, related to the human body, making the moon, as claimed by the Masters, the controller of generation.

It is a commentary on the intelligence shown by modern science when the moon, the feeblest of our luminaries, is selected as the only celestial body that has any definite effect on and relation to the earth. Science knows that the moon affects the tides of the seas, and in the same breath will disclaim any belief in the powers of other planets and celestial bodies, which are to the Moon as is the light of the Sun to a candle.

The Masters knew that as the Earth passes through the range of a Constellation, represented by a circle of 2,160 years, the Earth becomes subjected to the influence or vibrations of that particular Constellation; and we are able to determine the effect of the Constellations with infallibility by reason of the Sacred Animals, or traditional symbols, used with reference to their corresponding signs in the Zodiac.

Chapter No.5
Virgin Mother

We shall see, as we search back in the distant past, that the theological system was once a distinct Feminism. The symbolical god of that age was a Goddess without a husband, a Virgin who was the Cosmic Generatrix.

Definite traces of this have come down to us in the bible where it is said:

"Therefore shall a man leave his father and his mother, and shall cleave unto his wife; and they shall be one flesh" in that they shall be in perfect and harmonious vibration" (Gen.2:24). More ages pass, the earth moves into the influence of vibrations of other Constellations, and the Feminine principles begins to decline while the Masculine begins to increase. Definite traces of this face also appear in the bible, to-wit: "Thy desire shall be to thy husband, and he shall rule over thee" (Gen.3:16)

A space of many ages occurred between those two events recorded in Genesis.

Virgo

The Great mother; a goddess without a husband; the virgin who was the Generatrix, bearing the Divine Child, and reference to this time appears in the bible:

"Whosoever is born of God doeth not commit sin; for his seed remaineth in him; and he cannot sin. In this the children of God (Virgin Born) are manifest" (1 Jn. 3:9,10).

22

Virgo is the middle sign of the Earth Triplicity, the other two being Taurus and Capricorn. This was the last Golden Age of the Queen of Heaven that has some down to us in the bible. In that age the Goddess of the Full Moon ruled the propagative function of the world, and was the Mother of the Gods. The Chaldeans monarchs traced their descent from the Moon-God, which they regarded as the Mother Principle of Creation. Ages come and go, and the Mother Principle declines, like the waning of the Moon.

Came .the time when it appears the woman had degenerated to the point where help was necessary to aid in her function of production and she marries a man. Still her husband was a very minor object, and subject to her will, a fact recorded in the bible.

Leo

The cycle of Virgo began 13,216 BC, and ended 11,059 BC. Then the masculine commanding, fiery sign Leo came into power and extended until 8,902 BC.

Leo is the middle of the Fire Triplicity, the other two being Aries and Sagittarius.

Ages pass and Mother Principle continues to fade. The decline continues until the Mother Principle grows weaker than the Masculine, which now becomes the Positive Pole, and the Feminine the Negative, — the change resulting from the vibrations of the Constellation of Leo.

Cancer

The cycle of Cancer began 8,902 BC, and extended to 6,754 BC. This was the next step in the decline of the feminine. Cancer (crab) is the head sign of the Water Triplicity, and is called the paradox of the twelve signs of the zodiac. The other two are Scorpios and Pisces.

Gemini

Gemini is the head sign of the positive pole of the Air Triplicity, the other two being Libra and Aquarius, and this cycle extended from 6754 BC, to 4,588 BC, marking a further decline of the Feminine Principle.

The feminine vibrations during this period were slight on the spiritual plane and stronger on the physical, which tended to make woman material and give to man the major portion of Spirituality. A religion distinctly masculine is now born.

Taurus

This is the head sign of the positive pole of the earth Triplicity, the other two being Virgo and Capricorn. This cycle extended from 4,588 BC. to 2,432 BC.

The feminine principle continues to sink into materialism and was reduced to the astral desires, resulting in the expression of a strong development in the passions, and especially in the generative department. It was under the influences of the vibrations of Taurus, the bull, that the object of veneration was the Golden Calf mentioned in the Bible.

Aries

This is the Head Sign and Positive Pole of the Fire Triplicity. The Cycle extended from 2,432 to 276 BC.

The mother principles sinks to the lowest point, and is ruled almost entirely by the epithumetic nature, being regarded by man as little more than an instrument to serve his demands and satisfy his lust. The Masters ball the story:

"I will greatly multiply thy sorrow and thy conception; in sorrow thou shalt bring forth children; and thy desire shall be to thy husband, and he shall rule over thee' (Gen.3:16).

A period of 8,626 years elapsed from the end of the reign of Virgo to the beginning of the reign of Aries. In that long period of time man rose, under the influence of the masculine variations of the Cosmos, from his minor role stated in Gen. 2:24, to his major role indicated in Gen. 3:16. Under the reign of Aries, "the Lamb of God" became the object of adoration when, in its turn, it opened the equinox for 2,160 years, "to deliver the world from the wintery reign of cold, barrenness and darkness," as the ancients termed it in their annual "Christmas" celebrations on December 25.

Pisces

This is the last sign of the negative pole of the Water Triplicity. The cycle began 276 BC. and ended 1881 AD., and takes us to the very core of the secret doctrine of Hermes and his Magic Wand, our work in which we gave an interpretation of the Caduceus.

This was the cycle of the child in a certain mystical sense. From this time onward we see the Mother Principle begin slowly to rise from its long decline.

The history of modern times show the position of woman, wife and mother gradually growing more honorable. The cause of the changing condition is due to the radiation of the ruling Constellation.

Aquarius

This is the last sign of the Air Triplicity. It is an aerial masculine, fixed, rational, expressive, obeying sign, the Negative Pole of the Air Triplicity.

The earth entered the cusp of Aquarius about 1881 AD., and the cycle will extend to 4,037 AD. In its spirituality Duality it is the sign of the Divine Sophia (wisdom). The attributes being soul memory, and diffusive of knowledge.

In the Egyptian zodiac this sign is represented by a Divine Figure pouring a double stream of water from a vase. Water symbolizes the Productive Principle. "The waters brought forth abundantly, after their kind" (Gen. 1:21). The two streams symbolize the waters of the Spiritual Principle and the waters of the Physical Principle.

The cycle of Aquarius brings the Mother Principle into fuller manifestations; and it will continue to increase, reaching it speak in the Cycle of Virgo, which ends in 17,723 AD.

The new awakening of the Feminine Principle in a New Birth is a datum of scientific observation, as we have shown in our work titled *The Red Dragon*. The students of biology show that the Masculine Principle is decreasing in power, with a corresponding increase in the Feminine. That secret of Life the Ancient Masters discovered in the Stars and recorded it in the Zodiac. Paracelsus wrote:

"The body of a man is his Home; the Architect who builds it is the Astral World; the Carpenters are at one time Jupiter, at another Venus; at one time Taurus, at another Orion.

"Man is a Sun and a Moon and a Heaven filled with stars. The World is a Man, and the Light of the Sun and the Stars in his body. The ethereal body cannot be grasped, and yet it is Substance, because Substance means Existence, and without Substance nothing exists."

That kind of philosophy has been too deep for modern scientists; who believe that man is the product of Evolution, so the pooh-poohed it as ancient nonsense.

Recent discoveries are changing the picture. It is now known that everyone of the millions of electrons contained in the smallest object visible under the microscope, is continually acting upon and being acted upon by all the bodies in the universe.

Science now admits that each body is the center from which various kinds of control proceed by the means of vibrations in the ether, passing out to another body again and it itself.

There are other processes of control that can as yet be defined only as mental, the quality of which rises from a special grouping of electrons through which man's Mind appears to act.

This is the ancient science of astrology which, until now, modern scientists have termed heathenism superstition. Now it is Cosmic Radiation. That hard it is for modern scientists to admit that they are so far behind the ancient masters.

Great changes will occur in the centuries to come, and some of them are already here. Wonderful it would be to live through and witness the events that will take place.

Before that remarkable record was destroyed by the church, the Ancient Masters had a very complete history and chart, covering nearly half a million years, showing and describing the states and conditions of the earth and its inhabitants, as affected and influenced by the various signs of the Zodiac, or the Celestial Bodies which the signs represent.

It is said that Abraham had a large astrological tablet on which the fate of every man might be read. This information had been compiled from that ancient record.

Had we that record now, it would show what we may expect in the affairs of the world for ages to come. We would know that we are not living in the "latter days" as the clergy have been claiming for more than half a century.

Solar Center

One author says, "There is no spiritual designing in nature or in man without the power of the Sun." Man, the Microcosm, has a Solar Center just as the Macrocosm has a Solar Center. This Center is the great nerve plexus of the Sympathetic Nerve System, the largest of all the prevertebral plexuses, located behind the stomach, and also called the Abdominal Brain.

The name "Solar" was given to this center because it is recognized as the "powerhouse of the body, just as the Sun is the great powerhouse of our cosmic Solar System.

There are two nerve systems: The cerebro-spinal, consisting of the brain and spinal cord; and the sympathetic, over which the Abdominal Brain presides.

The sympathetic system consists of a series of ganglionic centers, expending or lying on each side of the spinal column from head to coccyx.

In ancient scriptures, the ganglia are called chakras, meaning whirling wheels. Forty-nine of them are enumerated, but the principal ones are the mystic seven, as follows:

1. Sacral ganglion (Muladhara);
2. Prostatic (Svadhisthana);
3. Solar plexus (Manipura);
4. Cardiac Anahata);
5. Pharyngeal (Vishuddha);
6. Thalamus (Ajna);
7. Crown of head (Sahasrara).

The Manipura (solar plexus) is the controlling center of the vital process of the body, and of the strange forces utilized in all systems of psychic or faith healing.

The Ancient Masters discovered certain subtle function and offices of the Abdominal Brain, and taught their disciples valuable methods of effectively employing its finer forces and hidden powers. They discovered that the Solar Plexus is the seat of the emotional nature of Man and that the part popularly held to be played by heart, is in reality performed by the Solar Plexus.

The Masters discovered that man consciously send messages to the Solar Plexus. Modern psychologists are making these discoveries, but give the Masters no credit, and make their discoveries appear new by giving new names to the processes.

The Abdominal Brain of the average man is in a state of semi-sleep, or more correctly; in a state of semi-consciousness resembling that of the somnambulist, who intelligently performs tasks without being full conscious thereof.

In cases of emergency, or of threatened danger of the body, the "instinctive mind" of the Solar Plexus does wake up; and, in such cases, manifests a far greater degree of consciousness than it normally expresses. The Abdominal Brain is the third seal up from the bottom of the seven seals of that mysterious Book, written within and on the backside, and sealed with seven seals (Rev. 5:10), which we have covered in our work, *"The Magic Wand."*

In Yogic literature, this Third Seal is the Manipura Chakra, "full of sparkling jewels, which lies in the Chitrini Madi, as beautiful as a chain of lightning and as fine as the lotus fiber."

One author writes. "When the Yogin opens this chakra, known as Fire Dharana (concentration), the killer of the fear of death, then 'fire cannot harm nor burn the Yogin.'" — Kundalini power. In the Bible, red horses and red dragons symbolize this seal. Zechariah saw a man on a red horse, and a chariot with red horses (1:8; 6:2).

In Revelation, when this seal was opened, a fiery-red horse appeared; to its rider was given a sword, and power to take away peace from the earth (Rev. 6:3,4)

As stated above, this seal is the Manipura Chakra, and its zodiac sign is Scorpio, the house of Mars, the War-God.

This region of the body is the seat of the epithumetic nature, the abdominal division represented by the red horse, and its rider is passion personified. He appears later in the allegory in the role of *The Great Red Dragon* that stood before the woman, ready to be delivered, for to devour her child as soon as it was born" (Rev.12:1-4), — a parable which we interpreted in our work titled *The Red Dragon*.

Chapter No.6
Majesty of God's Kingdom

Many chapters of Book of Psalms are nothing but Lyrics to the Sun, but when the church fathers prepared their bible they inserted false headings in these chapters, such as "The majesty of Christ's Kingdom," "An exhortation to Praise God," The Majesty of God's Kingdom." etc. (Ps.93,95,96,97,98, etc.)

The gods of the ancients were all nature-gods, and the Sun God was the highest, mightiest, and only true God (Jn. 17:3).

The Sun is man's greatest God today and will always remain such.

Man is searching for health and long life. He is pictured in health journals and periodicals with arms outstretched toward the Sun. He instinctively turns to the Sun as his only true God, knowing that if the Earth were cut off from their Solar Radiation for thirty days, all living things on the globe would become extinct, and the earth would become a barren, frozen waste.

Realizing these facts, the ancients endeavored to exhibit their appreciation of the Sun by erecting vast temples in the name of the Sun. Since the Sun did so much for them, how could they do less than to pay their highest respects, tributes and praises to the Shining Orb that made it possible for them to live and enjoy life.

The Sun was the Master and giver of Light and Life. It was the symbol of the animative and generative powers of the

Universe; for under the influence of the Sun's rays, they saw the naked trees put forth new leaves, and the barren earth grow green with luxurious vegetation.

The ancients regarded Sun Light as the power of animation. The essence of Light, the invisible Fire, developed as Flame manifested as Light and Heat.

The Sun was the monotheistic or collective symbol of all other gods. Being such, it was esteemed by them the most sacred of all sacred symbols.

Delaulanye wrote: "The Sun and Moon represent the two great principles of generation, the active and the passive, the initiative, and the receptive, the male and female.

"The Sun represents the actual Light. He pours his fecundating rays upon the Moon; both shed their light upon the offspring, the Blazing Star, or the Egyptian Horus, and the three from the Equilateral Triangle, in the center of which is the omnific letter of the Kaballa, by which Creation is said to have been effected."

It is the same in all ancient nations and all ancient religions. In his *Morals and Dogma of Freemasonry,* albert Pike wrote:

"The Moon was the symbol of the passive capacity of Nature to produce, being considered female, of which the life-giving power was the Sun. It was the symbol of Isis, Astarte, and Artemis or Siana.

"Zeus, the Son of Saturn, became the King of the Gods. Horus, son of Osiris (Sun) and Isis (Moon), became the Master of Life" (p.13)

Gold was freely used in the ancient temples because it was regarded as condensed sunlight. The Hebrew word for gold, Zahab, means Light, of which the Sun is the author. So, in the allegory of the Hebrews, the river Pison compasses the land of Gold (Light), and the river Gihon the land of Ethiopia (Darkness) (Gen. 2:11,13).

Spark of Life

We still speak of the Spark of Life. Science cannot invent a better term. The Spark that quickens the flesh, comes from the Sun, and so postulated by the Masters.

Long ages before the ancient Chaldean shepherds watched the Sun on their fertile plains, it ross regularly in the morning, like a fiery god, marched through the sky like a conquering hero, causing darkness to vanish and clouds to scatter, and they said that "a fire goeth before him, and burneth up his enemies, and the hills melted like wax."

The Sun sank out of sight in the west, like a majestic king retiring, only to return again in regular order in the same array of majesty. Man worships immutability. It was that regular, steadfast, immutable character of the Sun that men of antiquity worshipped.

The Sun for countless ages had seem thrones rises up and crumbles into ruin, and earthquakes shake the earth and topple over mountains. Beyond Olympus, beyond the Pillars of Hercules, he had gone daily to his abode, and returned daily again in the morning, to shine on the temples that men built to his worship.

The ancients personified the Sun as Brahma, Amon, Osiris, Bel, Adonis, Malkarth, Mithras, and Apollo; and the nations that did so grew old and died. Moss grew on the capitals of the great columns of his temples, and she shone on the moss. Bit by bit the material of his temples crumbled and fell, and still he shone on the crumbling ruins. The roof fell crashing to the pavements, and he shone in on the Holy of the Holies with unchanging rays.

Strange, indeed, it had been if men had not worshipped the Sun.

The Hindus called the Sun Kris. Khur, the Parsi word, is the literal name of the Sun. From Khur Khora, a name of lower Egypt. The Persians called the Sun Kuros.

In the ancient annals of Tsur, the principle festivity of Malkerth, the incarnation of the Sun at the winter solstice, held at Tsur, was called the re-birth of the Sun, or his awakening, and it was celebrated by means of a pyre, on which the Sun God was supposed to regain, through the aid of fire, a new life.

The festival was celebrated in the month of Peritius, the second day of which corresponded to our 25th day of December. Even the ancient calendar was changed by the church fathers in order to conceal and deceive.

Prof. Tyndal wrote: "We are no longer in a poetical but in a purely mechanical sense, the children of the Sun."

Napoleon said: "The Sun gives all things life and fertility. It is the true God of the earth."

John Newton, M.R.C.S, of England wrote: "The glorious Sun, the 'god of this world,' the source of Life and Light, was early adored, and an effigy thereof used as a symbol.

"Mankind watched with rapture the Sun's rays gain strength daily in the spring, until the golden glories of midsummer had arrived, when the earth was bathed during the longest days in his beams, which ripened the fruits that his returning course had started into life.

"When the Sun once more begin its downward course to the dreary winter solstice, his votaries sorrowed, for he seemed to sicken and grow paler at the advent of December, when his rays weekly reached the earth, and all Nature, benumbed and cold, sunk into a death-like sleep.

"Hence, feasts and fasts were instituted to mark the commencement of the various phases of the Solar Year, which have continued from the earliest known period under various names" (The Assyrian Grove).

Dunlap said: "The Sun gives life to all things, to all beings. Ani is the Sun, Ani-ma is the Life, the Soul; Ani-mare means to animate.

"Our very language today recognizes the Sun as the source of animation or existence.

"Sel or Asel (the Sun) is the source of Spirit, Seele. 'Soul' comes from 'sol'" (Spirt — *History of Man*, p.46).

Among the nations of Babylonia, Syria, India, Persia and Palestine, the word "As" means "life," and the Sun was called "As." The softened pronunciation of this word from "Ah"; for the "S" continually softens to "H" from Greece to India.

Ah is Iah, Ao, Iao. God tells Moses that his name is "I Am" (Ahiah), a reduplication of Ah or Iah. The word As, Ah, or Iah means "Life." The Assyrians and Persians called their chief God Asura, Ahura, As, and Assarac.

The Greek God, Saturn, is a compound of Ar, the Sun (Aries), Ur, Aur, Our, (to burn), and On, Ani, the Sun. The Sun God was the god of the waters, of fire and of life. Water was one of the four creative principles, as mentioned in our work *"The Mysterious Sphinx."*

Thales considered water the first principle in the formation of the world. It is so regarded in the Babylonian, Phoenician, and Egyptian cosmogonies, and in the first chapter of Genesis.

All was a moist mass, into which the Sun-God introduced Light, the creative principles and the principle of order and harmony, — the first cause of all animal and vegetal existence.

The Peruvian Viracocha, under the name of Con, is originally a Water-God, and the cause of all things. Sisuthrus, the Babylonian Noah, is the Sun in the sign of the Waterman in the Zodiac (Movers). The name is a compound of Asis in Edesa, the Sun.

Noah is the Aion of Nonus. Aioni the Sun with four wings, referring to the four seasons (Movers), the "first-born." He is Osiris and Adonis, two names of the Sun.

Osiris is both the Sun and the Inundation, and in this respect, is the same as Noh, the god of annual overflow of the Nile. In the Assyrian period the Hebrews worship the Sun, Moon, Planets, and all the host of heaven (2 k. 23:5). The Hebrew names Shemuel, Samael, Samuel, are composed of Sem or Shem, the Sun, and El, the Sun.

Isaiah puts in the mouth of the Babylonian king these words, "I will exalt my throne above the stars of God (El-Sun)" (14:13).

The ancient religion of China and India were the same as that which was universal in all parts of the world, viz., an adoration of the Sun, Moon, Stars and the elements.

All ancient religion worshipped Nature in some form; and in all ancient religions, the deepest and most awe-inspiring attribute of Nature is the Power of Propagation.

The most ancient writings of the Chinese, said to extend back in a direct line over 44,000 years, and containing many accounts of commerce ceasing because of the sinking of large islands and the rising of large continents from the sea, show that astronomy was not only understood by the Chinese of very remote times, but that it formed an important branch of state policy and the basis of public ceremonies.

Eclipses were accurately recorded which occurred thirty centuries before the gospel Jesus was ever invented; and the Confucian books continually refer to observations of the celestial bodies and the reflection of the calendar. The most ancient Chinese astronomers know precisely the excess of the solar year beyond 365 days.

Fire and Spirit

Solar fire controls, to a certain degree, not the equal the vegetal and animal kingdoms; and fire is the only element that can subjugate metals and stone, and reduce all things to invisible gases. Every living thing, consciously or instinctively, honors the orb of the day. The sunflower always faces the solar disk. There is in man a real Sun Center, — the Solar Plexus, a great nerve, ganglia, the largest of the prevertebral plexuses, located back of the stomach, and also called the Abdominal Brain. While the material composing the Earth was still in the Sun, it was in a fiery state. But as fire burns not the Spirit, man's existence was also in being at that time.

Man's astral body does not perform physical functions. He does not breathe, needs no air, and fire has no effect on him. He can go anywhere, as air, water and fire makes no difference.

The ancients believed that if a young woman walked naked through a field in the intense sunlight of midday, she would be the pregnant (Goldberg). They must have some good evidence on which to base that belief. Many ancient nations so revered the fire and light of the Sun, that they would not permit their altars to be lit by any other means than the concentration of the Sun's rays through these glasses and light the altar fires that had been prepared for this occasion.

The ever-burning lamp of the alchemist, which burned for thousands of years without fuel in the catacombs of Rome, is a symbol of the same spiritual fire within man's body.

This spiritual spark is an infinitesimal part of the Divine flame, the Cosmic Fire, from whose flaming heart the altar fires of all creatures have been lighted.

This fire built by man is a very small part of the Great Fire of the universe that produces life and generation. Just as it sustains life, it also generates life.

And just as it generates, so does it consume, transforming everything it touches into ashes and smoke under certain conditions. Fire is the beginning and the end of things.

Fire and Sun serve man as symbols of animative and generative force. The Sun is distant and cannot be touched. One cannot even look at it when it is at its zenith. It is difficult to visualize its actions on the earth, or to see in the concrete its generative quality.

Fire is intangible. The child tries to grasp the flame before him, but it only burns his fingers. As the Sun and Fire were represented by symbols, the time came with the masses when the Sun and Fire were almost entirely forgotten, and they worship the symbols as something more than symbols. The gods and saviors grew out of the symbols, and the Sun and Fire were entirely forgotten. All gods and saviors began as symbols of the Sun, then the Sun was forgotten and the gods and saviors became actual persons.

The Sun was personified in such divinities as Brahma, Mithra, Osiris, Adonis, and Jesus. Then the Sun was forgotten and these figures became real persons.

In his great work *"Science of Religion,"* Max Muller wrote:

"The Hebrews worshiped the Sun, Moon, Stars, and 'all the host of heaven.' El-Shaddai was one of the names given to the Sun of God.

"Parkhurst, in his 'Hebrew Lexicon' says, 'El was the very name the ancients gave to their god Sol, their Lord and Ruler of the hosts of heaven.' "El", which means 'the strong one in heaven' — the Sun — was invoked by the ancestors of all the semitic nations before there were Babylonians in Babylon, Phenicians in Sydon and Tyrus, before there were Jews in Jerusalem...

"Our ancestors learned to look up to the sky, the Sun, and the dawn, and there they saw the presence of a living power, half-revealed and half-hidden from their senses, — those senses which were always postulating something beyond what they could grasp.

"They went further still in their imagination. In the bright sky they perceived an Illuminator, in the all-encircling firmament an Embracer; in the roar of the thunder or the voice of the storm they felt the presence of a Shouter and of furious Strikers, and out of the rain they created an Indra, or a giver of rain" (pp.190,298).

In his work *"The Ancient City,"* M. De Goulanges said:

"The Sun, which gives fecundity; the Earth, which nourishes; the Clouds, by turns beneficent and destructive — such were the different powers of which the ancients could make gods. But from each one of these elements, thousands of gods were created; because the same physical agent, viewed under different aspects, received from men different names.

"The Sun, for example, was called in one place Hercules (the glorious); in another, Phoebus (The shining); and still again, Apollo (he who drives away darkness or evil). One called him Hyperion (the elevated being); another, Alexicacos (the beneficent); and in the course of the time, groups of men, who had given these various names to the Sun, no longer saw that they had the same god'" (p.162).

Chapter No. 7
The Sovereign Sun

In the 4th century A.D. Emperor Julian delivered an oration on the subject of the Sovereign Sun, and quoted at length from a treatise by Iamblichus on the gods, a work destroyed by the church, but excerpts from it are preserved in the writings of Proclus, a great philosopher.

According to the Proclus, the Great First Cause that supplies unites all things is called The One. The cautious powers of The One are called gods.

If we explore the one Monad of all mundane light, from which other lucid natures and sources of light derive their substance, we find that it is no other than the apparent obr of the Sun. "For this orbicular body," says Proclus, "proceeds from an occult and supermundane order, and disseminates in all mundane natures a light commensurate with each."

Proclus continues: "If we investigate the root, as it were, of all bodies, from which celestial and sublunary bodies blossom into existence, we may not improperly say that this is Nature, which is the principle of motion and rest to all bodies, and which is established in them, whether they are in motion or at rest.

"I mean by Nature, the one life of the world, which, being subordinate to intellect and soul, participates through these of generation. And this is more a principle that many and partial natures, but is not that which is properly the principles of bodies. For this contains a multitude of powers, and through such as are different, governs different parts of the universe.

"But we are now investigating the one and common principle of all bodies, and not the many distributed principles. Therefore, if we wish to discover this One Principle, we must raise ourselves up to that which is most united in Nature to its flower, and that through which it is a deity, by which it is suspended from its proper fountain, connects, unites and causes the universe to have sympathetic consent with itself. This one (Sun) is the principle of all generation, and is that which reigns over the many powers of Nature, over partial natures, and universally over everything subject to the domain of Nature."

At this point in his Oration, Julian, who believed he was the reincarnation of Alexander the great (p.6), presents an account of the nature of the Sun, excerpted from Proclus on Plato's Theology, and says, "The Sun is allotted a supermundane order in the world, an unbegotten supremacy among generated forms, and an intellectual dignity among sensible natures. Hence, the Sun has a twofold progression, one in conjunction with the other mundane gods, but the other exempt from them, supernatural and unknown...

"Aristotle said, 'Man and the Sun generate man,' making the Sun the common Father of all mankind. The sun existed from eternity without any generation, and will be eternal through all the following periods of time. The planets, dancing round him as their king, harmoniously revolve in a circle, with definite intervals, about his orb.... The light of the moon is increased or decreased according her distance from the Sun.

"We infer his (Sun's) perfective power from the whole phenomena, because he gives vision to visive natures' for he perfects these by his light, and has the capacity of connecting all things into one, form the properties of motion conspiring into union and consent. Also, he leads Souls on high, and elevates them to the intelligible world.

"The Solar God, with a sure measure motion, raises and invigorates as he approaches, and diminished and destroys as he recedes. He vivifies by his progress, moving and pouring into generation the River of Life. The Light, which flows from the Sun, will not suffer itself to be mingled with anything; nor is it polluted by any sordid nature, or by contagion; but it abides everywhere pure, undefiled, and impassive.

"The Sun is the cause of the secretion of forms and the concretion of matter. For the distribution of solar rays throughout the world, and union of light, exhibit the demiurgic secretion of the artificer.

"And lastly, the Sun being super-mundane, emits the fountains of Light; for among the super mundane natures there is a Solar World of total Light; and this Light is a Monad prior to the empyrean, ethereal, and material worlds.

Julian concluded his oration with this statement:

"Therefore, I earnestly entreat the Sun, King of the Universe, that He will be propitious to me for my affection of His divinity; that He will impart to me a good life; more perfect wisdom; a divine intellect; and a gentle departure from the present state (a physical existence) in a convenient time, that I may ascend to His Divinity, and abide with Him in perpetual conjunction." — (p.95).

In his Epistle to the Hebrews, Paul the apostle said: "Wherefore we receiving a kingdom that cannot be moved, let us have grace, whereby we may serve God acceptable with reverence and Godly fear: FOR OUR GOD IS A CONSUMING FIRE" (Heb. 12:29).

In his work, *"Back To The Sun,"* Charles Whitby, B.A., M.D., wrote: "All beings proceed from, and are comprehended in, the first being; all intellects emanate from one first intellect; all souls from one first soul; all natures blossom form one first nature; and all bodies proceeded from the vital and luminous body of the world.

"And, lastly, all these great monads are greatly comprehended in the Great One, form which both they and all their depending series are unfolded into light. Hence, the first one is truly the unity of unities, the monads of monads, the principle of principles, the God of Gods, one in all things, and yet one (the Sun) prior to all" (P.183).

Chapter No.8
Ab-Ram the Sun-God

For sixteen hundred years the clergy have preached the biblical story of Abraham from the "letter" of the scriptures. In the 4th chapter of his epistle to the Galatians, Paul clearly asserts that these "things" concerning Abraham "are an allegory."

The biblical scribe covered the story of the creation down to the flood of Noah is eleven chapters. He hurried on through chapters 10 and 11 as though anxious to begin a new narrative.

In these two brief chapters he covers a cast period of time, form the death of Nash, who lived after the the flood 350 years (Gen.9:28), down to the building of "great cities" in "the land of Shinar" (Gen.10:10-12), and to the birth of Ab-Ram in the land of "the Chaldees" (Gen. 11:26,28). A different order of procedure appears when Genesis XII is reached. In the first verse we read: "Now the Lord said to Ab-Ram, get thee out of thy country, and from thy kindred, and from thy father's house, and unto a land that I will show thee; and I will make of thee a great nation." Then fourteen chapters are devoted to Ab-Ram, and his family, and his work. Then his name is changed; "Neither shall thy name any more be called Ab-Ram, but thy name shall be called Abraham; for a father of many nations have I made thee" (Gen. 17:5).

That statement seems quite innocent according to the letter, but according to the spirit, it means much. What is meant by the statement, "For father of many nations have I made thee" (Gen. 17:5). Ab-Ram was a Chalean, not a Jew. He was born in Ur of the Chaldees. Ur was the home of his father, Terah, who begat Ab-Ram at the age of 70 (vs.26).

Ur was dedicated to and the chief seat of the Moon-God Sin, whence comes the name Mt. Sinai, to which God descended from heaven, in smoke and fire, and was there met by Moses and received the law (Ex. 19:18). Terah took his family and set out "to go into the land of Canaan; and they came unto Haran (Kharran — Acts 7:2), and dwelt there. Teran died there at the age of 205 (Gen. 11:32). Ab-Ram grew up in Haran, living there until he was 75, then "went forth to go to Canaan" (Gen. 12:4,5). Now we shall see who Ab-Ram is, and whence comes the name. S.F. Dunlap tells us in his *Spirit History of Man* (1858). He said:

"The fire-god of Ur was Ab-Ram...The Hebrew word Ab means father, and Ram (head sign of the zodiac) means Most High — Ab-Ram and Is-Ra-El were names of Saturn.

"Saturn-Kronos was highest God and Highest Planet; and he was also regarded as Time, the eternal Kronos that was before all things. (On the Babylian cylinders Saturn-Kronos carries the Ring of Eternity). "Ab meant father; Ab-Ram meant father on High; Bara meant Creator, and Ab-Ram, the Creator of the people (Am equals people). --P.75.

Ab-Ram, married, and the name of his "wife was Sa-Rai, concern which Dunlap said:

"Sahara is the moon...it was usual with the Old Arabians to regard Saturn and Ab-Ram as their progenitor; and while regarding Saturn as their father, they claimed Sahara (Asarah, Asherah Venus) as their Mother; for the Moon is the Mother of the Kosmos, and the poet wrote that 'all things are born of Saturn and Venus'....

"Ab-Ram, then, the father of the Arabs and the Hebrews — The Hebrews came from Hebron, hence their name — Hebers (Hebraioi) of Hebron (Khebron) — a fire of the Fire-worshippers of Sada". — P .76. During the many years that Ezra and his Jewish associates were in exile in Babylonia (Chaldea), they had lots of time to study these traditions, and thus discovered a legend among these ancient people to the effect that all great races and all great men were the descendants of certain gods.

So, in line with this legend, Ezra invented the story of Ab-Ram (Most High Father--Sun), and Sa-Rai (Moon-god), and he begins with the 12th chapter of Genesis, to have it agree also with the twelve Constellations, called the signs of the Zodiac thus having Ab-Ram connected with the zodiac. "For a father of many nations have I made thee" (Gen. 15:5), actually means that the Sun was regarded as the Generative Principle of the Universe; and so Ab-Ram, the Sun-God, was the "Father of Nations and Races."

The Moon was regarded as wife of the Sun; and Ezra has Hebrews descend as the children of Ab-Ram (Sun) and Sa-Rai (Moon). He then cleverly weaves a humanistic fable around these mythical figures, gives them the appearances of actual persons, has children born of them, gives them names, and they have children, some of which go down into Egypt, where they "increase abundantly and multiplied, and waxed exceeding mighty; and the land is filled with them," — in just a few generations (Ex. 1:7). Some heavy production. All allegory said Paul.

Egyptian records contain no account of any migration of "the children of Israel" into Egypt. There was no such migration. The story is a myth. The story of Ab-Ram is a myth. Abraham himself is a myth.

It was the work of the priest Ezra. He found that other races had histories, and so he invented one of his people, and exalted them by having them descend from the Sun and Moon.

For many centuries the clergy have delighted in describing Abraham's unbounded faith, when they related the fable of Abraham's willingness, at the command of the Lord, to offer his son Isaac as a burnt offering (Gen. 22:1-12). More allegory, as Paul said.

Here is a typical illustration of how the ancient scribe transformed his Sun and Moon, the progenitors of the race, into man and woman.

Chapter No.9
Christian Sun God

The Christian have their Sun God but know it not. Dupuis wrote: "All solar deities have a common history, which, summarized, is substantially as follows:

"The god is born about December 25, of a Virgin. For the Sun, entering the entering Winter Solstice, emerges in the zodiac sign Virgo, the heavenly Virgin. His mother remains ever-virgin, since the Sun's rays, passing through the zodiac signs, leave it intact. His infancy is begirt with dangers, for the new-born Son is feeble in the midst of the winter cold, fogs, and mists, which threaten to devour him. His life is one of toil and peril, culminating at the Spring Equinox in a final struggle with the powers of darkness. At that period, the day and night are equal, and both fight for mastery.

"Through the night veil the Sun and he seems dead; though he has descended out of sight below the earth, yet he rises (resurrection) again triumphant, and he rises in the zodiac sign of the sign of the lamb (Ram, Aries), and is thus the lamb of God (which taketh away the sins of the world, — Jn. 1:29), driving away the darkness and death of the winter months.

"Henceforth he triumphs, growing ever stronger and more brilliant. He ascends into the zodiac and there he glows "on the right hand of God," the very essence of the Father," the brightness of his glory."

Remsburg said: "Christ wears the livery of a solar god. His mother, the virgin, was the mother of the solar gods; his twelve apostles correspond to the twelve signs of the zodiac.

"According to the gospels, at his crucifixion, the Sun was eclipsed, he expired at sunset, and rose again with the Sun: the day appointed for his worship, the Lord's day, is the Die Solis, Sunday, of the Sun Worshippers; while the principal feasts observed in his memory, were one observed in honor of the Sun God" (The Christ, P.462).

Dr. G. W. Brown declared: "Strange as it may seem to some people Mithras and Osiris, Dionysos and Bacchus, Apollo and Serapis, and many others (including Jesus), in name all masculine Sun Gods, and all inter blended, a knowledge of one being a knowledge of all, wherever located and worshipped" (Researches in Oriental history).

The chief gods of ancient religions were not real personages, but personifications of the Sun. All of the gods and goddesses of the ancients, melt and merge into one another, and finally into one. For these god and goddesses were nothing more nor less than symbols of the powers and processes of the universe, and chiefly those of the Sun, expressed in many ways and by a multitude of names. Men in all ages have expressed in words, the thoughts and emotions aroused in them by varying phases of that great Globe of Light on which we, no less than they, depend for everything, including our life.

We can trace in the Vedic hymns, step by step, the gradual development that transforms the Sun from a mere Light to a Creator, Preserver, Ruler, Rewarder, Redeemer of the world. In fact, into the Supreme Being. That picture presents the literal truth; for the Sun is all that and more. The Sun sees everything, both good and evil, and becomes the ALL-Seeing-Eye (Job 28:10). It is true light, that lighteth every man that cometh into the world (Jn. 1:9).

1. The birth of the Solar Gods occur at early dawn on December 25. On that day the Catholic and Christian ceremonies of the Nativity are celebrated in Bethlehem and in Rome, even at the present time, early in the morning.

This day was considered by the ancient astronomers as the Sun's birthday. At the commencement of the Sun's apparent annual revolution round the Earth, it was said to have been born, and, on the first moment after midnight of December 24, all ancient nations celebrated the announcement of the "Queen of Heaven." the "Celestial Virgin of the Sphere," and the birth of the Sun God. On that day the Sun having fully entered the Winter Solstice, the Sign of the Virgin was rising on the eastern horizon.

On that day were born all the Solar Gods, — Krishna, Buddha, Osiris, Horus, Mithras, Bacchus, Tammuz, Apollo, Jesus, and all other religious personifications of the Sun.

The woman's symbol of this stellar sign was represented first by ears of corn, then with a newborn male child in her arms.

Volney wrote: "The first division of the first decan of the Virgin represents a Virgin with flowing hair, sitting in a chair, with two ears of corn in her hand, and suckling an infant called Jesus by some nations, and Christos in Greek" (Ancient Ruins, P.166).

In his work on Symbolism, Dr Thoman Inman presents this ancient symbol on the very first page of his book.

2. Jesus was born of a virgin (Matt. 1:23).

The virgin is the bright and beautiful Dawn, and Virgo is one of the Zodiac signs.

In Sanskrit, Ida is the Earth, and wife of Dyaus (sky), and so we have the mythical phrase, "the Sun at birth, as it rises in the east, rests on the earth." In other words, at birth the Sun is nursed in the lap of his mother. In the Vishnu Purana, Devaki, the Virgin Mother of Krishne, is called Aditi, which, in the Rig-Veda, is the name of Dawn.

In an Ancient Arabian manuscript in the Royal Library at Paris, is a picture of the Twelve Signs of the Zodiac. That of Virgo is a young woman, and in the Egyptian mysteries she was called Isis. Her representation, with a child (Horus) in her arms, exhibited in her temple, was accompanied by the inscription:

"I am all that is, that was, and that shall be; and the fruit which I brought forth is the Sun" (Pike, p.455).

3. The birth of Jesus was foretold by a star (Mat. 2:2,9,10).

The geography of the sky shows the chaste, pure immaculate Virgin, suckling an infant, preceded by a star, which rises immediately before the Virgin and child.

4. The heavenly host sang praises (Lu. 2:13).

All nature beams and smiles at the rebirth (resurrection) of the rising Sun, which sheds light in dark places, and arouses the sleeping vegetation from its winter slumber.

Glory to God in the highest, on earth, peace will toward men. The whole of the horizon is irradiate with joy. The spirits of the nymphs of heaven dance and sing. The Solar God is born, to give joy to the earth, peace to men, and sight to the blind and health to humanity.

5. Jesus was born in a Cave because there was no room in the inn (Lu. 2:7).

All solar gods and saviors are represented as being born in in a cave or a dungeon. This symbolizes the darkness from which the Sun rises in the morning.

"As the dawn springs fully armed from the forehead of the cloven sky, so the eye first discerns the blue dome of heaven as the first faint arch of light gleams in the east This arch is symbolized by the Cave which the infant is born."

6. Jesus visited by the "wise men from the east" (Mat. 2:1).

This is a logical, for the Magi, the "wise men from the east" were none other than the Sun-worshippers, and at early dawn on December 25, the astronomers of the Arabs, Chaldeans, Hindus, and other Oriental nations, greeted the "infant savior" with gold, frankincense and myrrh. They started to salute their God before the rising of the Sun (Ezekiel. 8:16), and having ascended a mountain (1.K. 3:2; 2 K. 17:32; 2 Chr.33:17), they waited anxiously for the rising of the new-born Sun, facing the East, and there hailed his first Glorious Rays with incense and prayer. The shepherds also, who remained in the open air watching their flocks by night, had a custom of prostrating themselves, and paying homage to their Sun-god. When the Sun rose, they wondered how, just born, he was so powerful, and greeted him with these words: "Hail, Orient conqueror of the Gloomy Night."

The human eye could not bear the brilliant majesty of him whom they called "The life, the Breath, the Brilliant Lord and Father." The poet of the Vedas observed:

"Let us worship again the Child of Heaven, the Sun of Strength, Arusha, the Bright Light of the Sacrifice. He rises as a Mighty Flame; he stretches out his wide arms; he is even like the wind. His light is powerful, and his (virgin) mother, the Dawn, gives him the best share, the first worship among men" (Huller's Chips, Vol.2, p.96,137).

Cox wrote: "As the hour of his birth drew near, the mother (Dawn) became more beautiful, her form (sky) more brilliant, while the dungeon (dark earth) was filled with glorious light as when Zeus came to Danae in a golden shower" (Arayan Hyth, vol.2, p.133).

At length the child is born (Sun rise), and a halo of brilliant light encircles his cradle (horizon), just as the Sun appears at dawn in the East, in all its splendor. His presence reveals itself there, in the dark cave (dark horizon), by his first rays, which brighten the countenances of his mother (Dawn), and others who are present as his birth. (When Jesus was born, on a sudden there was a great light in the cave, so strong that their eyes could not bear it.) — Protevangelion, Apoc. cj. 14.

7. Jesus was ordered to be put to death (Mat. 2:3).

All Sun-gods were fated to bring ruin upon the reigning monarchs (Darkness). Who is the dark and wicked Kansa, or his counterpart Herod? He is Darkness, which reigns supreme, but which must lose his power when the young Sun God of Light and Glory is born.

The new-born Sun scatters the Darkness; so the phrase went out among the multitude that the child was to be destroyer of the reigning monarch; and oracles and magi warned the latter of the doom in store for him; so the newborn child is ordered to be put to death by sword, or exposed on the bar hillside, — as the Sun seems to rest on the Earth (Ida) on its rising. Fisk said:

"The exposure of the child in infancy represents the long rays of the rising Sun, resting on the hillside" (Myths and Mythmakers, p.198).

Cox said:

"The Sun-god is exposed on the slopes of Ida (Earth). This is the rays of the newly-born Sun resting on the hillside. In Sanskrit, Ida is the Earth, and from this comes the mythical phrase, the Sun at birth is exposed on Ida — the hillside. The rays of the Sun must rest on the hill-side long before they reach the dells below" (Aryan Mythology, vol. 1. p.221).

8. Jesus was tempted by the devil (Matt. 4:1-11).

Temptation by, and victory over, the evil one, symbolizes the victory of the young Sun over the clouds of storm and darkness.

Rising up in obscurity, the Sun tries his first fight with Darkness, and is victorious. He shines without a rival. Clouds and darkness are round about him, but "a fire goeth before him, and burneth up his enemies round about." (Ps.97:2,3). Then having conquered his enemies, and being free from every obstacle, he set sail across the vast space of blue, his brilliant Disk with thousands of glorious rays melting the hills like wax, and "the heavens declare his righteousness, and all the people see his glory" (Ps. 97:5,6), while the whole world rejoices in his Light and Warmth.

The Sun God appears in all his glory, and in his sovereign splendor; he has attained the summit of his course; it is the moment of triumph. And "thou, Lord, art high above all the earth; thou art exalted far above all goods" ((Ps. 97:1-9).

9. Jesus raises the dead (Mat.9:25; Jn. 11:43).

The Sun is the source of life. As it awakens the Earth from Winter Sleep, and raided the dead vegetation to life, so the Sun Gods of all religions were raisers of the dead. When the leaves fall and wither on the approach of winter, the "daughter of the earth" would be referred to as dying or dead; and as no power but that of the Sun can raise the vegetation of the earth to life, this symbolical child of the earth would be represented as buried in sleep (hibernation), from which the touch of the Sun alone could arouse her.

10. Jesus heals the sick (Matt. 9:35).

As the sun raided the dead it also gives health to humanity.

11. Jesus walks on the water (Matt 14:25).

The rays of the Sun move over the face of the deep (Gen. 1:2).

12. Jesus is received in Jerusalem with cries of Hosanna (Mar. 21:9).

The whole earth smiles with joy and gladness at the coming of the newborn Sun, while millions welcome his brilliant rays.

13. Jesus calmed the wind and raging water (Mat. 8:26; Lu.8:24).

The rays of the Sun drive away the cloud of the storm and still the wild blasts of the wind and the foaming waves of the sea.

14. Jesus lighteth every man that cometh into the world (Jn.1:9). That is the common function of all Solar Gods.

15. Jesus glorified God on earth (Jn. 17:5). The Sun gloray-fies itself to all the people of the earth.

16. Jesus is betrayed by Judas and put to death on the cross.

The Sun, moving south, has now reached its extreme southern limit. His work for this season is done. The powers of Darkness and winter, which fled in the spring before his conquering march, have at last won the battle in the autumn, and the Sun is crucified in the heavens on the Southern Cross, a constellation containing eighteen stars so grouped as to form a cross. He is pierced by arrow of Winter. Before he dies, he sees his Twelve disciples, symbolic of the twelve months of the year, and the twelve signs of the zodiac.

Cox remarks;

"The crucifixion of the Sun-gods is simply the power of Darkness triumphing over the Lord the Light," and Winter conquering, Summer.

"It was at the Winter Solstice that the ancients wept for Tammuz (Ezek. 8:14), the fair Adonis, and the other Sungods, who were (symbolically) put to death, on the cross, by the boar, slain by the thorn of Winter" (Aryan Mythology, Vol.2, p.113).

17. Jesus foretold his death and resurrection (Matt. 17:21).

Throughout the fable, the Sun God performs his cosmic duty. These things are regular and must be; for that purpose, was he created. The suffering of death was an essential part of the mythos; and, when his hour was come, he must meet his dorm, as surely as the Sun, once risen, must pass across the sky, and sink into his sepulchre of darkness beneath earth and sea.

18. Many women were there beholding afar off (Mk, 15:40).

The Sun Gods forsake their homes and mothers, and travel through all the different countries doing good work.

Finally, at the end of their career, the mother is back by their side, to cheer them in their last hours. The dark mists were spreading over the sky, but still the Sun God sought to gaze upon the fair face of his mother, and comfort her.

"Weep not for me, my toil is done, and now is the time for rest. I shall come again in the bright land which is never trodden by the feet of Night" (Lu. 23:37-29).

(Note: Here the student should read our work titled *"Mystery Man of Christianity,"* in which is analyzed and explained the "Second Coming of Christ.")

19. There was darkness over all the earth. (Lu.23:44).

In the struggle against the dark clouds arrayed against him, the Sun God is finally overcome. In this manner ends the career of toll and sorrow of the Sun God.

After a long struggle against the approaching enemy, the Sun God sinks slowly down, with the ghastly hues of death upon his pale face, while none is nigh to cheer him, save the ever-faithful women.

Cox says: "It is the victory of the clouds over the dying Sun, which is to be seen in the legendary history of the Sun Gods" (Aryan Myth. vol. 2, p.91).

The three hours of darkness over the land, from the sixth to the ninth hour, represents the three cold, dreary months of Winter in the region of Egypt, Persia, Palestine and Babylonia, when the vegetation has shed its leaves and gone into its winter sleep, to be raised from the dead to life by the return of Spring.

20. Jesus descended into Hades.

This is the Sun God's descent into the lower regions in the Winter solstice. The Sun enters the sign Capricornus, the ill-omened He-goat, and the astronomical winter begins. The days have reached their shortest span, and the Sun his extreme southern limit. Arriving there, the Sun God is said to have been slain, and dragged down into the realm of darkness. For three days and three nights the Sun seems to stand still in the lower regions (Hell). The Sun God are made to "descend into hell" and remain there for three days and three nights in the bowels of the earth, symbolized by a fish, is made to say, "out of the belly of hell cried I, and thou heardest my voice" (Jonah 2:2).

Regarding the descent of Jesus into hell, Doane wrote:

"This was one of the latest additions of the Sun-myth to the gospel story of Jesus. This has been proven not only to have been an invention after the Apostles' time, but even after the time of Eusebius (AD 325).

"The doctrine of the descent into hell was not in the ancient creeds or rules of faith. It is not to be found in the rules of faith delivered by Irenaeus (AD 190), or by Origin

(AD 230), or by Tertullian (AD 210). It is not expressed in those creeds that were made by the Nicene, nor Constantinopolitan; nor in those of Ephesus, nor Chaldeon; nor in those confessions made at Sardica, Antioch, Selencia, Sirmium, etx." (*Bible Myths,* p. 494, ft. note).

21. Jesus rose from the dead and ascended into heaven (Luke. 24:6).

Resurrection from the dead and ascension into heaven are solar features, and were symbolized in the Ancient Mysteries. At the Winter solstice the ancients wept and mourned for the Son God, slain by the cruel power of Winter, — and on the third day they rejoiced at the Resurrection of their Lord of Light.

After remaining stationary three days and three nights in the lower regions, from December 22nd to the 25th, the Sun rises triumphantly over the powers of Winter darkness, and begins to ascend northward in the heavens — thus he "rises from the dead," as it were, and 'ascends into heaven," to redeem the earth and its people from the cold and gloom of Winter, which; in the exoteric religion of the ancients, was symbolical of sin, evil, and suffering; as the Summer was an emblem of joy, happiness, and immortality.

The early church fathers sought to give a Christian significance to the ancient rites which they copied from so-called paganism; and the mourning for Tammuz; the fair Adonis (Ezek. 8:14), and the joy of the ancients at the rising of the resurrected Sun, became the joy of the Christians at the "resurrection" of their Jesus.

The festivals of the Resurrection of the Sun God were generally held by the ancients on March 25, when the awakening of Spring may be said to result from the returning of the Sun from the lower regions, to which he had departed in his autumnal course.

At the Equinox, the Vernal, at Easter, the Sun has been below the Equator, and suddenly rises above it. It was dead to those north of the Equator, who invented Christianity, but now it exhibits a Resurrection and an Ascension to heaven,

Bonwik wrote:

"The church, at an early date of its career, selected the ancient festivals of Sun worship for its own, ordering the birth of its Jesus, at Christmas, at a fixed time, and the resurrection at Easter, a varying time, is in all ancient religions; since, though the Sun rose directly after the Vernal Equinox, the festival, to be correct in the ancients' point of view, had to be associated with the New Moon" (*Egyptian Belief,* p.182).

Doane said:

"Throughout the whole legend, Jesus is the toiling Sun, laboring for the benefit of others, and doing hard service for a thankless and cruel generation.

"Watch his Sun-like career of brilliant conquest, checked with intervals of storm, and declining to a death cloud with sorrow and derision. He is in constant company with his Twelve Apostles, the Twelve Signs of the Zodiac.

"At this birth the evil of Darkness attempts to destroy him. Temptation to sloth and luxury are offered him in vain. He has his work to do (Luke 2:49), and nothing can stay him from doing it — as nothing can arrest the Sun in its journey through the sky.

"Like all solar heroes, he has his faithful women who love him and the Marys and Marthas here play of the part. His toils are but a thousand variations of the drama of the Ancient Mysteries of the great conflict that the Sun Gods wage against the demon of darkness.

"As the Sun awakens the Earth to life when winter is gone, so Buddha, Osiris, Tammuz, Adonis, and Jesus were raisers of the dead. When the leaves fell and withered on the approach of Winter, the 'daughter of the earth' would be regarded as dying or dead, and, as no other power than that of the Sun can raise vegetation to life, so the touch of the Sun brings her back to Life."

22. John the Baptist decreases while Jesus increases.

According to the Christian calendar, the birthday of John was on the day of the Summer Solstice, when the Sun begins to decrease. How true to the course of the Sun then are the words attributed to him in the John gospel, when John says that he must decrease and Jesus increase (Jn. 1:27-30).

Chapter No.10
Lamb of God

23. Jesus was the Lamb of God, which taketh away the sins of the world (Jn. 1:29).

The worship of the constellation of Aries (Ram, old lamb) was the worship of the Sun in its passage through the zodiac sign of Capricornus. By the ancients this Constellation was called the Lamb of God which taketh away the sins of the world.

Inscribed in the most ancient tombs of Egypt, Greece and Rome was the worship of the Lamb; and the figure of a Lamb appeared on the Christian cross until the year AD 680, when the Sixth Council of Constantinople finally adopted, after a long debate, a religious symbol that was thought to be the least known, which was the figure of Prometheus dying on a cross instead of on a rock.

When the new symbol appeared, the form was that of Prometheus, but the head and face were those of Apollonius of Tyana, who became *The Great Mystery Man of the Bible*, as explained in our work of that title.

From this decree, the identity of the Christian worship of the Sun, the zodiac Lamb, is certified beyond the shadow of any doubt and the mode by which the ancient worship was propagated is clearly shown.

Nothing could more plainly prove the existence of a general practice than a written order of a council to regulate it.

The worship of the Constellation of Aries is mentioned by Foane as follows:

"This constellation was called the Lamb of God by the ancients. He was also called the Savior of the world, and was said to save mankind from their sins. He was always honored with the appellation of Dominus or Lord and called the Lamb of God, which taketh away the sins of the world. The devotees addressed him in their litany, constantly repeating the words, "O Lamb of God, that taketh away the sins of the world, have mercy on us. Grant us thy peace" (Bible Myths, p.504).

The church applied to Jesus the monogram of the Sun, IHS, which was the astronomical and alchemical sign of Aries, Ram, Lamb; and, in short, there was nothing in the ancient religion that was not applied to him.

Constantine the Great, father of the Roman Catholic Church, had on his coins the figure of the Sun, with the legend: "To the invincible Sun, my companion and guardian," as being a representation, wrote King, "either of the ancient Phoebus, or the new Sun of Righteousness, equally acceptable to both Jews and Gentile, Pagans and Christians, from the double interpretation of which the type was susceptible" (Gnostics, etc. p,49).

Jesus is represented with a halo of golden light surrounding his head, a florid complexion, long golden hair, and a flowing robe.

In the same manner was represented all the Sun Gods, from Krishna of India to Baldur of Scandinavia. By a process of metaphor, the rays of the Sun were changed to golden hair, to spears and lances, and to robes of light.

Manly Hall wrote:

"In that age during which the vernal equinox occurred in Aries, the solar divinity was represented as a golden haired youth holding in one hand a lamb, and a shepherd's crook in the other.

"Thousands of years before the birth of Christ the pagans adored this figure of life and beauty. On the day the equinox, they gathered in the squares before their temples, crying out as with a single voice: 'All hail, Lamb of God, which taketh away the sins of the world ...

"In Aries the Sun was called Chrishna, from which, probably, the Greeks formed their Krios, a ram, from the Chaldee, Kresa, a throne, or seat of power, in allusion to the power of the Sun when in Aries, his exaltation" (story of Astrology, p.109).

In Egyptian mythology, Osiris was the personification of the Sun. The power of Osiris was symbolized by an Eye over a Scepter. The Greeks termed the Sun the Eye of Jupiter, and the Eye of the World; and his is the All-seeing Eye in Freemasonry.

The Oracle of Claros styled him King of the Stars and of the Eternal Fire that engenders the year and seasons, dispenses rain and wind, and brings daylight and darkness.

Osiris was invoked as the God that dwells in the Sun and is enveloped by his Rays, the invisible and eternal force that modifies the sublunary world by means of the Sun.

24. Jesus is to be the judge of the quick and the dead (2 Tim. 4:1)

Osiris, as a personification of the Sun, was to be the Judge of the dead. He is shown on Egyptian monuments, seated on his throne of judgement, bearing his staff, and carrying the Crux Ansats, which the Egyptologists called the "Symbol of Life." It represents the male triad and the female unit. There are few symbols more commonly met with in Egyptian art than this.

All the Sun Gods were judges of man's deeds, seeing, as the Sun does, "from his throne in Heaven," all that is done on earth.

The Vedas mention Surya, the pervading and irresistible luminary, as seeing and hearing all things, noting the good and evil deeds of man.

The East

The Sun rises in the east, and "at the door of the temple of the Lord, between the porch and the altar, were about five and twenty men, with their backs toward the temple of the Lord, and their faces toward the east; and they worshipped the Sun toward the east" (Ezek. 8:16).

Thousands of years before that passage was written, men had "worshipped the Sun toward the east." Thousands of years after our body has disintegrated and returned to the gases of the air, men will worship the Sun.

The Freemason unconsciously betrays the origin of his doctrine when he "looks to the east." For the east is the place of the Rising Sun, which rules and governs the day.

As we study Sun Worship we understand why the word East appears so often in the Holy Bible, Helios Biblia, Sun Book.

God planted a garden eastward in Eden; and there put the man whom he had formed (Gen. 2:8). He drove out the man and placed at the east of the garden Cherubins, and a flaming sword which turned every way, to keep the way to the Tree of Life (Gen. 3:24). Then Lot chose him all the plain of Jordan; and Lot journeyed east (Gen 13:11).

Every Freemason travels east, searching for "more Light" (Ronayne's *Hand-book of Freemasonry,* p.123). Balak the king of Moab hath brought me from Aram, out of the mountains of the east (Num. 23:7). Ab-Ram, the Sun God, gave gifts, and sent them away from Isaac his son, while yet lived eastward, unto the east country (Gen. 25:6).

Their windows, and their arches, and their palm trees, were after the measure of the gate that looketh toward the east; and they went up unto it by seven steps (Ezek. 40:22). The Seven Steps Symbolized the Seven Sense Powers of Seership.

He brought me to the gate that looketh toward east; and behold, the glory of the (Sun) God of Israel came from the way of the east; and the earth shined with his glory (Ezek. 44:9). There came wise men from the east to Jerusalem (Mat. 2:1). I saw another angel ascending from the east (Rev.7:2).

Tertullian said that the Christians were taken for Sun worshippers because they prayed toward the east, after the manner of those who adored the Sun (and did not try to conceal the object of their worship).

When a Manichaean Christians came over to the orthodox Christians, he was required to curse his former friends as follows:

"I curse Zerades (Zoroaster) who, Manes said, had appeared as a god before his time among the Indians (Hindus) and Persians, and whom he calls the Sun.

"I curse those who say that Christ is the Sun, and who pray to the Sun, and who do not pray to the true God, only toward the East, but who turn themselves round, following the course of the Sun with their innumerable supplications. I curse those who say that Zarades and Budas and Christ and the Sun are all one and the same" (*Bible Myths,* p.503).

And so we see that from the very first the Christians have been charged with being Sun worshippers, yet trying to conceal the real nature of their supplications.

25. Jesus was a Fisher of Men (Matt. 4:18,19).

After being 2,160 years in the sign of Aries, the celestial rotations caused the vernal equinox to occur in Pisces, and during that period Jesus appeared as the Fisher of Men (Matt. 4:18,19). The fish that was the earliest symbol of Jesus, and that symbol appears on all the ancient Christian monuments. This was because the Fish was another emblem of the Sun.

Jonah was swallowed by a big fish, and was in its belly three days. (John 1:17).

Abarana wrote: "The sign of his (Christ's) coming is the junction of Saturn and Jupiter, in the sign Pisces" (Quoted by King: The Gnostics, etc. P. 136).

The preserving god Vishnu, the Sun, was represented as a Fish, and so was the Syrian Sun God Dagon, who was also Preserver and savior.

The fish, as a symbol of the Sun, was sacred among many ancient nations, and may be seen on ancient monuments, showing that everything in religion centers at last in the Sun.

26. Jesus washes the feast of his disciples (John 13:5-10).

Being actor on the cosmic stage of Life, Jesus is made to play his dramatical part right down to the last letter of his piece.

As the Zodiac sign Pisces affects the feet of the Microcosm, so Jesus, representing this sign of the zodiac, is presented in the Bible as washing the feet of his disciples.

27. Jesus to come a second time (John 14:2,3).

"In my Father's House are many mansions; if it were not so, I would have told you. I go to prepare a place for you. And if I go and prepare a place for you, I will come again, and receive you unto myself; that where I am, there ye may be also."

On the basis of this statement, one Christian author wrote:

"There is no fact in history more clearly established then the fact of the "First Coming' of Christ. But as His 'First Coming' did not fulfill all the prophecies associated with His 'coming,' it is evident that there must be another 'coming to fulfill them completely." The doctrine of the "millennium" designates a certain period in the history of the world, lasting a long, indefinite space (vaguely a thousand years, as the word 'millennium' implies, during which the kingdom of Christ Jesus will be visibly established on the earth.

The unanimity of the early Christian teachers exhibited in regard to 'millenarianism' proves how strongly it had laid hold of the imagination of the church, to which, in the early stage, immortality and future rewards were to a great extent the things of this world as yet.

Not only did Cerinthus, but even the orthodox doctors — such as Papias (Bishop of Hierapolis), Irenaeus, Justin Martyr and others, delighted themselves with dreams of the glory and magnificence of the millennial kingdom.

Papies, in his collection of traditional sayings of Jesus, indulged in the most monstrous representations of the rebuilding of Jerusalem, and the colossal vines and grapes of the millennial reign.

According to the general opinion, the millennium was to be preceded by great calamities as a sign of its coming, after which Jesus would appear, and would annihilate the godless heathens, or make them the slaves of the faithful, overturn the Roman empire, from the ruins of which a new order of things would spring forth, in which 'the dead in Christ' would rise, and, along with the surviving saints, enjoy an incomparable felicity in the city of the "New Jerusalem," mentioned in the Bible as "coming down from God out of Heaven." (Rev. 21:2).

Finally, all nations would bend their knee to Jesus, and acknowledge him only to be the real Christ — his religion would reign supreme.

The doctrine of the millennium and the second advent of Christ Jesus has been an important one in the Christian church. The ancient Christians were animated by a contempt for their present existence, and by a just confidence of immortality, of which the doubtful and imperfect faith of modern ages cannot give us any adequate notion.

In the primitive church, the influence of the "Second Coming" was powerfully strengthened by an opinion, which, however much it may deserve respect for its useful and its age, has not been found agreeable to experience. It was universally believed that the end of the world and the kingdoms of heaven were near their hand.

The clergy have been preaching for years that "we are living in the latter days."

In the year of 1000 AD, the expectation of the "last day" reinvented the doctrine with a transitionary importance; but it lost all credit again with the hopes, so keenly excited by the crusades, faded away before the stern reality of Saracenic success, and the predictions of the "Everlasting Gospel," a work of Joachim de Floris, a Franciscan abbot, remained unfulfilled.

After the devotees and followers of the new gospel had, in vain, expected the Holy One who was to come, they at last pitched upon St. Francis as having been the expected one, and, of course, the most surprising and startling miracles were said to have been performed by him.

Some of the fanatics who believed in him, maintained that he was "wholly and entirely transformed into one person of Christ," and maintained that the gospel of Joachim was expressively preferred to the gospel of Jesus.

As stated above, in our work titled *Mystery Men of the Bible* we have explained the underlying astronomical facts and features of the statement "I will come again," and shown how a falsehood is and the false are so intricately and delicately interwoven that it is absolutely impossible for the unprepared mind to separate the one from the other.

The Bible is a book that has gone out to the world and chained in darkness and ignorance a larger number of people than any other book has done, and those people must live in that darkness and error until they evolve to such mental ability that they can winnow the true from the false in this book and come to understand its falseness.

Chapter No.11
Perfection

We have shown in another work that *The Great Red Dragon* mentioned in the Bible symbolizes, in its broadest sense, the Principle of Desire in all its various gradations, from the vaguest yearnings and mere promptings of the body's appetites, down to the grossest phases of passion and lust.

Man's superior intellectual powers give him complete domination over the entire world not only, but also over himself. But he lets his desires and appetites drag him down from that exalted plane of Master to a state of abject slavery.

Ignorance of the purpose of Life creates desire, and knowledge creates disappointment. For knowledge shows that Desire indicates mental deficiency, and experience shows that gratified Desire produces weakness that destroys.

That is the reason why the ancient Masters said, "speaking generally of occult literature, acquaintance with it is most disappointing, because all such Literature promises too much in comparison with what it gives. (Ouspensky, p.193).

The reason of the disappointment is obvious. Desire is an artificial creation that cannot be satisfied, as men possesses within himself all things in the universe. For all things in the Macrocosm are contained in the Microcosm.

Instead of man's realizing this fact, and making the best and proper use of what he has, he neglects his grand possessions in his searchings for more.

Gratification of desire produces disillusionment. For it fails to bring the pleasure anticipated: And the pleasure resulting is temporary, while the damage done is permanent. According to the Ancient Masters, and confirmed by ages of sad experience, the greater the pleasure derived through the physical, the greater damage done to the Spiritual. No better example of this great truth can be found, than in the secondary lasting effects of copulation and masturbation, which keep the world filled with feebleminded physical wrecks.

The pleasure of ephemeral, while the damage is eternal. It means suffering permanent damage for fleeting pleasure, — a fact that caused Paul (Pol) to shout, "Flee fornication — He that committeth fornication sinneth against his own body — It is for man not to touch woman (1 Cor. 6:16, 7:1).

He that seeketh pleasure through the physical, pays dearly for it through the spiritual. So the Masters wisely observed celibacy and asceticism.

Fools look without for blessings and pleasure, but the wise look within. Fools believe that they have a glorious home "above", but the wise know they are always home. For the kingdom of Heaven is within, not without (Luke 17:21).

The less man uses and indulges, the more perfect he grows. He gains in Perfection as he gains freedom from desire. The more he yields to desire and appetite, the more he inclines from Perfection. The whole problem is summed up in the term Self Denial. "If any man will come after me (Perfection), let him deny himself and follow me" (Matt. 16:24). In other words, perfection grows out of self-mastery. Man changes his world as he changes himself. In that day for such man a new Universe is created (Rev. 21:5). For the external world changes.

In every man, however fallen and degraded he may be, are contained all the forces, both cosmic and deific, which brought him into being: and these forces but await the time when the resurgent Divine Life again stirs within him, and then they begin a new evolution, the work of making perfect the Lord of the whole earth (Gen. 1:26,27,28: Zech. 4:14).

Total self-denial in all things is perfection. The less man needs the more complete he becomes. He gains the perfection he craves as he gains freedom from all desires. The more he desires, the less complete he is and the farther he inclines from perfection.

He that overcometh all desires and masters himself, shall inherit all things good in life; and I (Perfection) will be his Guide, and he shall be my son; and I (Perfection) will bless him and lead him to good health and long life in his own right, as the reward he has earned (Gal. 6:7, Rev 21:7). — Amen.